THIS JOURNAL BELONGS TO:

_____

Self-Esteem Journal

**Encouraging Prompts and Practices
to Nurture Your Self-Worth**

BRIANA HOLLIS, LSW

ROCKRIDGE
PRESS

Interior and Cover Designer: Diana Haas
Art Producer: Meg Baggott
Editor: Samantha Holland
Production Editor: Ruth Sakata Corley
Production Manager: Jose Olivera

Paperback ISBN: 978-1-63807-420-5
R0

Contents

*The thing that is really hard, and really amazing,
is giving up on being perfect and beginning the work
of becoming yourself.*

—Anna Quindlen

Introduction

Hi there! My name is Briana Hollis, and I'm so happy you decided to pick up this journal. As a licensed social worker and life coach for nearly a decade, I've been working with people of all ages to help support their educational and personal goals, and an important part of this is helping them build up their self-esteem.

Even as a social worker and life coach, I'm not immune to self-esteem issues. For a long time, I hated my legs, and this greatly affected my self-esteem. I thought they were too short and too big. I wanted them to be long and shapely, like what you'd see in magazines, movies, and television. Because of this, I would never wear shorts or skirts; instead, I wore long pants and jeans, even in the middle of summer!

One summer when I came home from college, I decided to challenge myself to wear shorts at least once a week, especially out in public. What happened? Nothing super significant, but I did learn that my legs were just legs. They allow me to go from here to there; precisely what they were made to do. Do I love my legs now? Not always. But I have a lot more compassion for myself when I don't.

This is often where self-esteem begins: learning to accept things as they are and then moving toward love and appreciation. This doesn't mean you won't have bad days, but you'll come to understand that those bad days won't last forever.

We all deal with self-esteem issues from time to time. Self-esteem is your overall internal sense of value and worth that is separate from how others might value you. It's powerful for a lot of reasons, including feeling good about yourself. Researchers have found that healthy self-esteem can lead to better health, lower levels of depression, and greater overall success in life.

You know you have a lower sense of self-esteem if you:

- Think that others are better than you

- Have a fear of failure

- Are unable to remove yourself from unhealthy relationships or situations

- Are unmotivated to try something new

- Only focus on your weaknesses

  But if you have healthy self-esteem, you may be able to:

- Feel confident in yourself and your identity

- Create healthy boundaries

- Understand your areas of strength and needed improvement

- Have a positive outlook on life

- Feel secure in your life and relationships

Which, if any, of the listed healthy or unhealthy characteristics do you find in yourself?

A lower sense of self-esteem is thought to be mostly tied to life experiences. It can also come from factors like age, physical and intellectual abilities, race and ethnic origin, education, career, or genetics.

For example, a life experience like being bullied as a child or teenager could have a significant effect on your self-esteem. This was the case for me: I was bullied from elementary school until I graduated high school. It had a very significant impact on my self-esteem. Because I was bullied, I had a hard time connecting with others. I felt unwanted by my peers and undeserving of the friends that I did have. This feeling carried on into adulthood, and I still struggle with relationships.

One of the things that has helped me the most in my self-esteem struggle is journaling. I started when I was young and continue to journal to this day. It enables me to untangle all the thoughts in my head. Seeing them on paper gets them out into the world (even if I'm the only one that sees them) and allows me to recognize patterns so I can mitigate issues when they come up.

This journal will help you objectively evaluate your self-esteem and work toward building it up through powerful and engaging prompts and exercises, positive affirmations, and inspiring quotes. No matter where you are regarding your self-esteem, you will gain transformative knowledge by working through this journal.

Working on your self-esteem (or any personal development goal) is a personal journey. While this journal has been written so each section builds upon the previous one, how you use it is up to you. You may find one section more helpful than another on a given day; feel free to skip around, depending on what feels right to you in the moment.

Journaling is a fantastic way to work through your feelings; however, this journal is not a replacement for ongoing assistance from a mental health professional, medication, or medical treatment. If you have depression, anxiety, or any other mental health issue, finding a professional that you can trust can be incredibly helpful in your healing. There is no shame in seeking support when you need help. I've done it many times throughout my life. In the Resources section on page 158, you will find information to help you locate a therapist in your area, if you choose to do so.

Building up your self-esteem (and keeping it up) will lead to discovering who you are. With each day, you can make small choices or take new, bold actions to continue that journey. The prompts and exercises in this journal are just the start, and you'll take it even further. Let's get started. I believe in you!

Self-Esteem Questionnaire

Before we get into the prompts and exercises, let's get an idea of where you are in your self-esteem journey. Rate the following questions from 0 (strongly disagree) to 5 (strongly agree).

1. I feel confident in who I am as a person.

    0   1   2   3   4   5

2. I understand and learn from my failures.

    0   1   2   3   4   5

3. I believe I am capable of achieving the goals I have for myself.

    0   1   2   3   4   5

4. I clearly communicate my needs and wants with others.

    0   1   2   3   4   5

5. I believe that I can grow and change.

    0   1   2   3   4   5

6. I am willing to try new things.

    0   1   2   3   4   5

7. I can have healthy relationships with people I care about.

    0   1   2   3   4   5

8. I believe that my thoughts and feelings matter.

0   1   2   3   4   5

9. I am proud to be the person that I am.

0   1   2   3   4   5

10. I feel optimistic about my life.

0   1   2   3   4   5

Now add up your scores. If you scored:

0–10: You've probably had a few experiences that deeply affected your self-esteem. Let's start creating a foundation to make it better.

10–20: It can take work to build up your self-esteem, and it may feel like you'll never get there. The good news is that you have a solid foundation to work with.

20–30: You may feel confident in some areas but less so in others. Let's work on building the tools and skills you need to feel confident, no matter what you're doing.

30–40: You're well on your way! You probably just need a few more tools to be where you want to be.

40–50: You've been able to cultivate a healthy sense of self-esteem. Keep going on your journey to strengthen your self-esteem even further!

To be beautiful means to be yourself. You don't need to be accepted by others. You need to accept yourself.

—Thich Nhat Hanh

Embrace Who You Are

Embracing who you are is not always easy, especially if you've spent the majority of your life trying to be someone you're not. We've all been told that we need to be this or that to be accepted. These messages may have come from our parents, friends, television shows, or society at large. The reality is, trying to be something we aren't will only lead to frustration, sadness, and low self-esteem. Conversely, embracing who we are, even when it's difficult, will lead to better outcomes in all areas of our lives, helping us cultivate better relationships, careers, hobbies, and everything in between.

In this section (and throughout this journal), we'll slowly work our way through all the layers that make you uniquely you. We'll explore how to shed the parts that aren't authentic—like the things we might say or do to please others—and start looking toward the parts that bring us joy and make us who we are. Whether your layers are like those in a cake, parfait, or onion (because onions are awesome, too!), you deserve to embrace who you are.

Embracing who you are also means shedding the layers of who you feel you're "supposed to be." What have others told you or implied that you're supposed to be? Have you told yourself any of these things? Is this person who you actually are or want to be?

_____

_____

_____

_____

_____

_____

_____

_____

_____

_____

_____

_____

_____

_____

Growing up and being who you are through your formative years isn't easy. What piece of advice would you give to your younger self about embracing who you are? Think about your younger self as a child or teen. What do you think they need to hear?

_____

_____

_____

_____

_____

_____

_____

_____

_____

_____

_____

_____

Explore Your True Self

Sitting with our own thoughts can often reveal our true selves. Let's explore.

1. Find a comfortable spot where you can sit in silence without distractions. If you live with other people, you may want to tell them that you need some quiet time.

2. For 10 to 20 minutes, just sit alone with your thoughts—set a timer if that helps. Try not to make any judgments on whether your thoughts are negative or positive. Let them come as they are and leave as they are.

3. Afterward, use the space below to reflect on the thoughts that came up during this exercise.

_____

_____

_____

_____

_____

_____

Part of embracing who we are is being grateful for everything we have been, are now, and will become. Gratitude journaling can help clarify some of the things that we like about ourselves. Below, write down at least five things about yourself that you are grateful for. For example, you could say, "I have a beautiful smile." Feel free to come back to this page whenever you need a reminder to embrace who you are.

_____

_____

_____

_____

_____

_____

_____

_____

_____

_____

_____

_____

The thoughts we have every day greatly impact how we feel about ourselves. This inner dialogue (whether it is critical or uplifting) is often ingrained in us as children. Throughout the day, carry this journal with you and write down any thoughts that you have about yourself in the space provided. Try not to censor them. What do you notice about your thoughts?

_____

_____

_____

_____

_____

_____

_____

_____

_____

_____

_____

Release Expectations

On page 2, we talked about the layers of you that don't actually fit who you are. Now let's see how we can release those parts—the parts that you believe your family, friends, or society want you to be. Think about the expectations and assumptions others have of you.

When you're ready, grab some paper and write all these parts down. Next, get rid of them in any way that you see fit. Rip up the paper and throw the pieces in the trash or recycling, scribble all over them until you can't see them anymore, etc.

Those things no longer represent who you are. You are your own person, and you get to decide who you want to be.

Oftentimes, we need to feel secure and safe in order to feel like we can be who we really are. What do safety and security mean to you? What steps can you take to feel safe? For example, you could join an online community that you identify with, or you can disengage with people who don't accept who you are. What other steps can you take?

_____

_____

_____

_____

_____

_____

_____

_____

_____

_____

_____

Box Breathing

Thinking about our self-esteem can get overwhelming, especially when we're first beginning to explore it. This is normal—there's a lot to think about and work through. A great way to move through the feeling of being overwhelmed is to practice a deep breathing technique. One of the most efficient deep breathing techniques is called box breathing. Give it a try:

1. Breathe in for a count of four seconds.
2. Hold for a count of four seconds.
3. Breathe out for a count of four seconds.
4. Hold for a count of four seconds.
5. Repeat steps 1 through 4 as necessary.

Come back to this exercise as needed whenever you're feeling anxious or overwhelmed.

A fun way to embrace who you are is to think about what animal encompasses your inherent traits. Are you assertive like a snake or hardworking like a bee? Describe the animal that you feel you are most like and its traits in the space below. The next time you're feeling low, think about this animal and all the amazing traits you have in common.

_____

_____

_____

_____

_____

_____

_____

_____

_____

_____

_____

We can learn more about who we are by thinking about how we like to spend our time. If we could plan the most uplifting and inspiring day, it would include a lot of what makes us truly happy. What would this day encompass for you? What would you do? Who would be there with you? Visualize exactly how it would go and write about it in the space below. What does this rewarding day tell you about who you are?

_____

_____

_____

_____

_____

_____

_____

_____

_____

_____

_____

_____

*Because true belonging only happens when
we present our authentic, imperfect selves to the world,
our sense of belonging can never be greater than
our level of self-acceptance.*

—Brené Brown

When we are trying to be someone we're not, we may engage in things we don't actually want to do. For example, you might have played baseball because your parents loved it instead of playing piano, which you were passionate about. What hobbies or activities are you interested in trying now that you are working on embracing who you are? Write them down, and plan on trying one of these hobbies or activities this week.

_____

_____

_____

_____

_____

_____

_____

_____

_____

_____

_____

Brain Dump

This exercise allows you to just write for a predetermined amount of time. It helps get all your thoughts out on paper so they don't take up space in your head. This is a great way to release thoughts that may be nagging you or bringing you down—it also can help you identify patterns in your thinking.

1. Grab a notebook and pen.

2. Set a timer for 10 minutes to do some brain dumping about you and who you are. Write about whatever you're thinking, without judgment.

3. What patterns or connections do you see? What resonates with you?

If this practice feels good to you, try to do it at least once a week.

By embracing who we are, sometimes we may fear losing someone or something we love by turning away from what we aren't. For example, if you told a parent that you don't actually like a shared hobby, you might lose a sense of closeness with them. If you embraced who you are and discarded what you aren't, what might you lose? How might you remedy the loss? For example, could you explore a new hobby with that parent?

_____

_____

_____

_____

_____

_____

_____

_____

_____

_____

_____

Our childhood is usually when we experience our truest selves. We cry when we're sad; we roar like dinosaurs when a silly mood strikes us. This could be because we haven't been told yet by society or people in our lives that we shouldn't do these things. How can you get back to that place of living your truth authentically? If you could do anything, what would your inner child do right now?

_____

_____

_____

_____

_____

_____

_____

_____

_____

_____

_____

_____

*I embrace my past and
my imperfections.
They make me who I am.*

Have you ever come home from work or school, or have been out with a group of people and felt completely exhausted? When we're not embracing who we are, it feels like we're putting on a performance. Not being who you are is draining! When was the last time you felt like you were putting on a performance? How can you work on being yourself and not an "actor"? What could you do differently?

_____

_____

_____

_____

_____

_____

_____

_____

_____

_____

_____

Grounding Exercise

On page 9, box breathing was introduced to calm any anxieties that arise when you're exploring your self-esteem. Another method of getting into a calmer headspace is called "grounding." Grounding can be done in many ways, such as counting the number of specific items in a room or naming different household items. Another easy way to practice grounding is through your five senses.

1. Find a quiet place where you can relax.
2. Look around and observe your surroundings.
3. Take a deep breath and practice grounding through your senses:
   - Name five things that you can see.
   - Name four things that you can touch.
   - Name three things that you can hear.
   - Name two things that you can smell (or two scents you like).
   - Name one thing you can taste (or one thing you like about yourself).

Sometimes our loved ones are spot-on in their descriptions of us, and other times it seems they don't know us at all. How do you think your family members and friends would describe you? Are these accurate depictions of who you are? How can you take steps to reconcile who you are with who they think you are?

_____

_____

_____

_____

_____

_____

_____

_____

_____

_____

When was the last time you felt on top of the world? For instance, you might have been dancing the night away or captivated by the sunset at a beach. During that experience, you were most likely embracing yourself, savoring the opportunity to celebrate with people, or being a part of a beautiful natural phenomenon. Describe your experience in the space below. How can you re-create moments like this more often?

_____

_____

_____

_____

_____

_____

_____

_____

_____

_____

_____

Favorite Things

What we own can tell us a lot about who we are or who we want to be. Go into the room in your home that makes you feel most like yourself. What do you notice about the items in the room?

_____

_____

_____

_____

Now choose three items that are most "you." These could be items that remind you of how you look, your personality, your values, etc. Write about why you resonate with each item.

Item 1: _____

_____

Item 2: _____

_____

Item 3: _____

_____

Our dreams, hopes, and desires can give us a peek into who we truly are or strive to be. List some of your hopes, dreams, and desires. Nothing is too big or small to be included here. After you've completed your list, refer to this page as a reminder whenever you need a boost of inspiration to keep being who you are.

_____

_____

_____

_____

_____

_____

_____

_____

_____

_____

_____

Living authentically can come with its own set of fears, like what others will think or if we're truly being who we are. This is completely normal and it happens to just about everyone. What troubles you most about embracing who you are? What steps can you take to move forward despite your fear?

_____

_____

_____

_____

_____

_____

_____

_____

_____

_____

_____

_____

_____

Creatively You

In this section, we've covered many things that make you uniquely you! Now it's time to get creative. In the space below, draw the things that make you who you are. These can be drawings of actual physical things (like a picture of yourself or the items that you listed on page 22) or representations of intangible elements of you (like your love of singing).

If your compassion does not include yourself, it is incomplete.

—Jack Kornfield

Lean into Self-Compassion and Self-Respect

Self-compassion and self-respect are two essential ingredients in building better self-esteem. We'll be exploring your own definitions of self-compassion and self-respect soon, but in a nutshell, self-compassion involves being gentle and kind with yourself, whereas self-respect involves honoring yourself and living according to your values.

Without these two components, you might be unable or unwilling to do the harder things that come with building self-esteem, like creating boundaries. You're only able to create boundaries when you know you deserve to be treated with respect (more on this in section 5 on page 105).

Leaning into self-compassion and self-respect may make you a bit uncomfortable. That's okay! Prioritizing yourself can feel like you're taking away from others, but you'll soon learn you're not. Being uncomfortable lets us know for sure that we're getting outside of our comfort zone.

Get comfortable living outside of your comfort zone, even if it is just for a brief period of time. But also know that it's okay if you need to step back, recharge, and come back later. That's leaning into self-compassion and self-respect right there.

Self-respect means something different to everyone. It can even mean something different at different times. Right now, what does self-respect mean to you?

_____

_____

_____

_____

_____

_____

_____

_____

_____

_____

_____

_____

_____

Every behavior we engage in shows something about who we are and what we believe. What are behaviors you engage in that show you respect yourself? Are there any behaviors that show a lack of respect for yourself? Now that you have this list, is your definition of self-respect the same as it was from the previous prompt? Go back to that prompt and revise it if necessary.

_____

_____

_____

_____

_____

_____

_____

_____

_____

_____

_____

_____

Self-Care Box

Creating a self-care or self-comfort box is a small way that you can lean into self-compassion. A self-care box is a small container of things that you can use when you're trying to be a little kinder to yourself.

To create one, gather items that bring you comfort, such as a favorite stuffed animal, photo, journal, souvenir, scent, or candle. Whatever you choose is fine. Depending on the items that you put in your box, you can use them in whatever way works best for you. For instance, if you put in a journal, you could write about what you're grateful for or do a brain dump (page 14). If you include a candle, you might light it while you meditate.

Whenever you need to practice some self-compassion, bring out your box and let yourself feel all your feelings.

You don't have to wait until New Year's Eve to make a resolution. A resolution is just a decision to do or not do something. What's at least one resolution that you can make to lean into self-compassion or self-respect? An example of a resolution might be to take a nap when you're tired because that's what your body needs. Create a plan to incorporate your resolution into your life.

_____

_____

_____

_____

_____

_____

_____

_____

_____

_____

_____

Just like self-respect, the definition of self-compassion and how it works in action is different for everyone. What does self-compassion mean to you? How do you see self-compassion showing up in your life? For example, it might look like you turning your phone on silent while you sleep.

_____

_____

_____

_____

_____

_____

_____

_____

_____

_____

_____

_____

Self-Soothing Touch

Humans crave physical touch. This can be a hug from a family member or a high five from a co-worker. One thing about physical touch that we don't often consider is how we practice self-soothing touch on ourselves. When you achieve something, do you ever pat yourself on the back? When your stomach is upset, do you give it a gentle massage? Do you ever comfort yourself by giving yourself a hug?

Think about all the ways you can care for your body through soothing touch. How can you be kinder and gentler in this area of your life? For the next week, practice caring for yourself through self-touch methods that comfort you. Reflect on how it felt for you, and continue with what helped you the most.

We all have simple pleasures that we indulge in from time to time. But sometimes we may think that we haven't earned these pleasures. This way of thinking is not in line with self-compassion. Below, list all the simple pleasures that you enjoy and why you enjoy them. When you're feeling like you don't deserve a simple pleasure, come back to this list and choose one to do anyway.

_____

_____

_____

_____

_____

_____

_____

_____

_____

_____

_____

There are moments in our lives when we feel incredibly proud of how we handled ourselves. We may have walked bravely into a situation or come out of one with our head held high. When was the last time you felt a great sense of self-respect? What were you doing, and what made that moment so impactful?

_____

_____

_____

_____

_____

_____

_____

_____

_____

_____

I strive to continuously treat myself with kindness, respect, compassion, and love.

Your name is a huge part of who you are. Use your name to speak kindly and respectfully to yourself. In the space below, write your name vertically. Pick a positive word to describe yourself using each letter. For example, my name would be B = Brave; R = Responsible; I = Inspiring; A = Adorable; N = Nice; A = Accomplished. How do you demonstrate each quality? Revisit this list often to build on your self-respect.

_____

_____

_____

_____

_____

_____

_____

_____

_____

_____

Random Acts of Kindness

Doing kind things for others can make it easier to do kind things for ourselves. Today, try to practice random acts of kindness. These acts don't have to be extravagant or take a lot of time or money. They can be as simple as paying for someone's coffee. Other ideas for random acts of kindness include:

- Offering to babysit someone's children
- Providing snacks and drinks for delivery workers
- Leaving a review when you've received good customer service
- Congratulating someone on an accomplishment

What are some other random acts of kindness you can think of? What is one that you can do today? Afterward, reflect on how it made you feel.

Leaning into self-compassion requires us to be kind to ourselves. This can take many forms. How can you be kinder to yourself tomorrow? You could take a break during work, go for a long walk after dinner, or give yourself some compliments. How can you work on being kinder to yourself on a regular basis? List some ideas, and then choose one to follow through on.

_____

_____

_____

_____

_____

_____

_____

_____

_____

_____

_____

Sometimes speaking to ourselves kindly and with respect is hard. It can be made easier by thinking about what we might say to a friend. Think of yourself as you do a loved one. What would you tell them on their journey to lean into self-compassion and self-respect?

_____

_____

_____

_____

_____

_____

_____

_____

_____

_____

_____

Listening to our physical and emotional needs is important when trying to lean into self-compassion and self-respect. Often, we ignore the signals that we should be listening to. Take some time to intentionally listen to your feelings. What do you need more of today? This could be sleep, time, love, connection, etc. How can you provide yourself with more of that?

_____

_____

_____

_____

_____

_____

_____

_____

_____

_____

_____

Role Models

One way that children learn is by modeling others. If our parents, siblings, or others in our lives, behaved a certain way, we're more likely to behave similarly. Even now as adults, we can use this tool to our advantage in building self-compassion and self-respect by looking to role models in these areas.

Begin evaluating your family members, friends, and others on how they practice self-respect and self-compassion, both in person and via social media. You may find that you are being bombarded with messages and behaviors that are the opposite of your goals. If that's the case, find a couple of people that you see exhibiting positive messages and behaviors and pay closer attention to them.

If you're not sure where to start, head to the Resources section (page 158) for some uplifting people to follow on social media.

Self-compassion is simply giving the same kindness to ourselves that we would give to others.

—Christopher Germer

When we think about holding grudges, it is usually us holding a grudge against some-one else. Grudges can often hurt us more than others because we waste our emotional energy on them. But sometimes we are holding a grudge against ourselves! What's one of the biggest grudges that you are holding against yourself? How can you forgive your-self and move forward?

_____

_____

_____

_____

_____

_____

_____

_____

_____

_____

Forgive Yourself

We've all done things that, in retrospect, were not in line with our values or the way that we want to present ourselves to the world. This is expected and a part of being human. Another part of being human is to show compassion and forgiveness. Today, take some time to make peace with yourself for past mistakes, hurts, or wrongs. Forgive yourself for past actions in the lines below.

I forgive myself for _____

I forgive myself for _____

I forgive myself for _____

I forgive myself for _____

I forgive myself for _____

You have some pretty fantastic qualities! Write about at least three extraordinary qualities that you possess and how they can help you on your journey to increase your self-esteem. Try to make using these qualities part of your day as you continue your journey.

_____

_____

_____

_____

_____

_____

_____

_____

_____

_____

_____

Emotional Baggage

Low self-esteem can be an issue because of things that happened in your past. They might have been things that you saw or did, or things that were done to you. This is sometimes referred to as our "emotional baggage." These are the things that we carry with us day to day, year to year.

We can only lay down this baggage and move forward once we recognize it and begin to heal. Start by recognizing what you're carrying. What weighs you down? What keeps you from rising up to your emotional potential? On a separate piece of paper, write it down, and then draw a suitcase around those words (or two or three). We'll continue to work on laying down this "baggage" and moving forward through the rest of this journal.

Small, simple changes in our behaviors and mindset can greatly change our life. If you practiced leaning into self-compassion and self-respect every day, where would you see yourself in the next two years? What would you be doing? Who would you be? How would you feel? Imagine these scenarios and write about it in the space below.

_____

_____

_____

_____

_____

_____

_____

_____

_____

_____

_____

_____

There will be times when you feel yourself leaning away from self-compassion and self-respect. What can you do to get yourself to lean back in? For example, you can take a few deep breaths, make a list of your positive qualities, or revisit some of these prompts and exercises. Write your best ideas. When you're in those moments, circle back to what you wrote down here.

_____

_____

_____

_____

_____

_____

_____

_____

_____

_____

_____

_____

Self-Compassion Roadblocks

There are plenty of roadblocks in the way of self-compassion and self-respect. Even though you may encounter many roadblocks, there are many ways to get past them. Below, draw the roadblocks that might be in your way. Consider your "baggage" (page 47) and other issues. Beside each roadblock, write down ways you can move past it.

Learning about self-compassion and self-respect is a never-ending journey. You'll learn something new every day of your life just by living, but you can also take charge and actively seek out knowledge. In what ways can you continue to learn about leaning into self-compassion and self-respect? To get started, check out the Resources on page 158.

_____

_____

_____

_____

_____

_____

_____

_____

_____

_____

_____

_____

Instead of letting your hardships and failures discourage or exhaust you, let them inspire you. Let them make you even hungrier to succeed.

—Michelle Obama

Welcome Failure as an Opportunity

Everyone, and I mean everyone, fails at something at some point in their lives. It is inevitable, but it doesn't have to make you feel like your world is crashing down around you. That feeling comes from your inner critic telling you that failure or mistakes are wrong. But that is not true. You don't have to be perfect. You will fail at something. And it will be okay. In fact, when we fail, we often learn something new that makes us better human beings.

To face failure with grace may require you to let go of memories and past actions that created emotional distress. This emotional distress can resurface without your being aware of its roots. For instance, you may dislike public speaking because you were laughed at during a talent show in grade school. It may not seem like there's a connection, but subconsciously, it's there.

In this section, we'll explore how to turn a failure into an opportunity to grow and become stronger. I know you've got it in you!

Everyone has a different idea of what it means to fail. It could be not meeting a goal, making a mistake, not being on time, or something else. What does failure mean to you? After you write about what failure means to you, think about how that definition changes your feelings toward it. What you might have seen as a failure before may no longer seem like a failure after you've defined it.

_____

_____

_____

_____

_____

_____

_____

_____

_____

_____

_____

There are many reasons why we might fail at something. We may have even helped the failure happen by participating in self-sabotage. This is completely normal, especially if you're working on your self-esteem. You may not feel like you deserve the achievement. In what ways have you perhaps practiced self-sabotage? How could you stop this from happening again?

_____

_____

_____

_____

_____

_____

_____

_____

_____

_____

Gentle Movement

Thinking about the times we've failed can be difficult. Being in a moment when we think we might fail is difficult, too. In those moments, it can help to focus on the present. One of the best ways to do this is by focusing on your body instead of your thoughts. Practicing gentle body movement can help calm any overwhelming feelings you are experiencing in the moment.

1. Wiggle your toes for a few seconds.
2. Take the movement into your legs. Stretch them in a way that feels good and natural for you.
3. Bring the movement to your torso. Take some deep breaths and feel your stomach rise and fall.
4. Next, wiggle your fingers and stretch your arms in a way that feels comfortable.
5. Lastly, gently roll your head in a circle a few times.

Come back to this exercise anytime you feel yourself losing focus on the present moment.

Sometimes a loss (losing a job, ending a relationship, etc.) can feel like a failure, but there are almost always lessons or opportunities that come with loss. What is something that you recently lost? What lessons can you take away from this loss? Reflect and write about the possibilities that may come from this experience.

_____

_____

_____

_____

_____

_____

_____

_____

_____

_____

_____

Our inner critic's voice is probably the loudest when we've failed at something. Think about a time that you failed. What did your inner critic tell you? Did you believe it, or were you able to override the self-criticism? How did you make that voice fade away? If silencing your inner critic is hard for you, check out the exercise on the next page.

_____

_____

_____

_____

_____

_____

_____

_____

_____

_____

_____

Name Your Inner Critic

We all have an inner critic. This voice tells us not to speak up when we feel we should, or shames us when we make a mistake. Naming our inner critic gives us an easier way to call them out when they're trying to make us feel bad. Our inner critic isn't the best version of us—they are an unwelcome trespasser—so they don't deserve our name. What's a fitting name for your inner critic? Negative Nina? Debra Downer? (I call mine Kevin.)

Name: _____

Now let's practice hushing them. Try saying these statements out loud, or come up with your own words:

(NAME), now isn't the time for you to be speaking.

(NAME), I'm going to do my best, no matter what you say.

Thanks for your thoughts, *(NAME)*, but I'm going to do this anyway.

Some failures continue to weigh on us, no matter how small they are or how long ago they happened. What is one failure that is still weighing on you, and what makes it different from other failures? What can you learn from this failure in particular? Putting old failures to rest can sometimes be as easy as reflecting on them and their lessons.

_____

_____

_____

_____

_____

_____

_____

_____

_____

_____

_____

There is resiliency in failing. The more you fail at something, the more you learn about how to do that thing and the more you learn about yourself. To show that you're resilient even in the face of failure, list three times that you continued to try something after failing. Anytime you're feeling down, use this prompt to remind yourself that you are resilient and failure isn't final.

_____

_____

_____

_____

_____

_____

_____

_____

_____

_____

_____

Constructive Feedback

Our inner critic criticizes us when we fail or make mistakes—sometimes it even criticizes us when we are trying to provide feedback to someone else! Has your inner critic ever said, "Who are YOU to provide them with feedback?"

Providing feedback and constructive criticism is as important as taking it. Well-chosen constructive feedback is valid and can be crucial to someone's growth.

The next time you're able to provide someone with appropriate feedback, do it—with detail. Saying, "Great job!" while nice, is not constructive. What did they do a great job on? What have you learned because of what they did? Try working up to providing people with constructive feedback at least three times a week. Reflect on your experiences with providing feedback and receiving it. As you continue to provide feedback, it will likely be easier to receive it, too.

Any failures I experience are
stepping-stones
to a new perspective.

We can't travel to the past, but we can reflect on it and learn from it. Take some time to think about a particular failure that you believe you could have changed had you done something differently. What would you have done differently? If you had done those things, what do you think would have happened instead?

_____

_____

_____

_____

_____

_____

_____

_____

_____

_____

_____

Silencing your inner critic by providing evidence against whatever it is saying. Write down one of your common inner critic comments. It could be that no one thinks that you're funny or you're not good at your job. (None of these comments are true, by the way.) Now list all the evidence that you have against that comment. The next time your inner critic gets too loud, remember this prompt and fire back with all the reasons they're wrong.

_____

_____

_____

_____

_____

_____

_____

_____

_____

_____

The Gift of Failure

We've reflected on how failure is an opportunity. Let's take it a step further and think of failure as a gift. Failure can reveal things you may not have otherwise learned about yourself and the potential good things that came of it. That's important. Think of some of the gifts that your failures have brought you and list them below. These gifts can be lessons, unexpected positive results, learned traits, or something else. Look back at any of the prompts if you need a reminder of what you've written so far. Finish off with an affirmation that sums up this lesson, such as *I have gained wisdom and discovered my resiliency through my failures.*

Failure: _____

The gift that came from it: _____

Failure: _____

The gift that came from it: _____

Affirmation: _____

Reframing a situation is a powerful way to change our perspective on it. Below, write about a situation that challenged you, such as having a difficult conversation with a loved one, or trying to overcome a shortcoming like procrastination. How could this situation be reframed in a way that's helpful to you? For example, *I shared my feelings even though I was unsure about the outcome.* After reframing this situation, write down what you learned from it.

_____

_____

_____

_____

_____

_____

_____

_____

_____

_____

_____

While working to embrace who we are, we get messages from all around us about what failure is, when we've failed, and how we should feel when we fail at something. We get these messages so often we may internalize them, which shows up in our inner critic. What messages have you gotten about failure and where do you think they came from? Are they accurate? Can you challenge them?

_____

_____

_____

_____

_____

_____

_____

_____

_____

_____

_____

One of the biggest reasons many of us are afraid of failure is that we're scared of the criticism that may follow. That criticism may come from our inner critic or people who witness the failure. How does the fear of being criticized fit into your narrative of failure? What could the criticisms teach you (whether they are valid or not)? Sometimes criticism can provide helpful feedback.

_____

_____

_____

_____

_____

_____

_____

_____

_____

_____

_____

A Fiery Perspective

Fire is a beautiful metaphor for failure. Sometimes when we fail, we feel like things are "going up in flames." But we can also consider that fire also provides warmth and light that can guide us as we move forward.

1. If you have a candle, light it. Alternatively, visualize yourself lighting a candle.

2. Let the flame represent your past failures and mistakes. Consider that once it is lit, you can't change the way it burns or how much wax is melted.

3. Bask in the candle's light and warmth. These are the lessons that you can take with you—your guiding light.

4. Spend as much as you need to meditate and reflect on this moment.

5. When you're ready to blow out the candle, thank it for providing a new perspective that you can carry with you.

And now go and make interesting mistakes, make amazing mistakes, make glorious and fantastic mistakes. Break rules. Leave the world more interesting for your being here.

—Neil Gaiman

Life presents us with countless opportunities. When we have an opportunity to do something, we can say yes or no. Sometimes we say no because we think we might fail. We don't even give ourselves the chance to try. When was the last time you said no to an opportunity because you feared that you would fail? How can you use this reflection to say yes next time? Write your thoughts in the space provided.

_____

_____

_____

_____

_____

_____

_____

_____

_____

_____

_____

Kind Words

We are almost always our own harshest critics. Your inner critic tells you everything you've done wrong at the least opportune times. However, your inner critic would never say those things to someone that you care for.

Think about a person you love or admire. If they made a mistake or failed at something, what would you say to them? Write it down on a separate piece of paper. I'm guessing you spoke kindly to your loved one and empathized with their experience.

The next time you experience failure or make a mistake, think back on this exercise and speak kindly to yourself just like you would to a friend.

The idea that we have to be perfect can be pervasive. You might have experienced the need to be perfect at home, at work, or in a friendship. Being perfect is not possible, and that's perfectly okay. Where does the need for perfection show up in your life? How can you challenge the idea that you need to be perfect?

_____

_____

_____

_____

_____

_____

_____

_____

_____

_____

_____

In the last prompt, we talked about the need for perfection and that it is not possible. While you don't have to be perfect to reach your goals or to succeed, it's helpful to be aware of your weaknesses or shortcomings. What are your shortcomings? Once you've identified them, what can you do to work on them or lessen their impact?

_____

_____

_____

_____

_____

_____

_____

_____

_____

_____

_____

It's said that every cloud has a silver lining. So think about this: Have you ever had a failure in your life that seemed devastating at the time, but then turned into something extraordinary or into a greater opportunity? How did it turn out, and what did you learn from it?

_____

_____

_____

_____

_____

_____

_____

_____

_____

_____

New Growth

Throughout this section, you've learned about yourself and how previous failures can be a springboard to growth. Recognizing and celebrating how you've grown is essential. That's what this exercise is about.

In the space below, draw a picture that represents your newfound growth. Get creative about what growth looks like to you, whether it's a flower, a branching tree, a child growing into an adult, or whatever speaks to you! Have you released any baggage? How does this feel as part of your growth?

You're beautiful, just the way you are. Shine on. And dare anyone to turn off the lights.

—Mandy Hale

Nurture Your Self-Worth

You've already taken some significant steps in your journey to building up your self-esteem. Pat yourself on the back, give yourself a high five, and celebrate the gift of being you. You've earned it!

But our work is not done; in fact, building self-esteem and nurturing yourself is a lifelong journey. Once you begin it, you'll wonder why you weren't doing it before. How you nurture yourself is different for every person. The key is to develop practices that support your overall happiness and well-being.

The following prompts and exercises will help you nurture yourself by learning how to speak more kindly to yourself, let go of negative thoughts, and find ways to celebrate your wins. Nurturing yourself is important for building your self-esteem because it helps you steer away from negative thoughts, comparing yourself to others, or repeating past negative experiences. When we focus on ourselves in kind and loving ways instead of harmful ones, we open the path to transformative growth and healing.

The word "nurture" can mean something different to everyone, and we all have different ways that we nurture other people and ourselves. What does being nurtured mean to you? Where does your definition of nurture come from? Think about the emotional, spiritual, and physical possibilities.

_____

_____

_____

_____

_____

_____

_____

_____

_____

_____

Rewire Your Brain

It's normal to have negative thoughts about yourself sometimes. It happens to everyone at one point or another, and it's nothing to be ashamed of. The good news is that your negative thoughts can be transformed into positive ones by retraining—thus literally rewiring—your brain. In the chart below, write down some of your negative thoughts about yourself. Then turn those negative thoughts into positive ones.

NEGATIVE THOUGHT	POSITIVE THOUGHT
EX. *I'M LAZY BECAUSE I SPEND TOO MUCH TIME LYING IN BED.*	*I LISTEN TO MY BODY WHEN IT NEEDS TO REST.*

Making a point to take care of yourself is hard if you've never really thought about it. For inspiration, think of a time when you nurtured someone or something else—a pet, a child, a friend, a plant, or even a project. What things did you do to help them feel happy, loved, and comforted? How can you translate those things to work for yourself? Alternatively, think about what you crave. How can you provide more of what you crave yourself?

_____

_____

_____

_____

_____

_____

_____

_____

_____

_____

_____

Part of nurturing yourself is taking care of your physical body. Our body does so much for us, but we often procrastinate on measures to stay healthy. Think about any aches, pains, or unaddressed issues that you need to work on healing. Write them down here, along with a plan to take steps to feel better. This could include joint pain, dental issues, dry skin, weight loss or gain, or any other message your body is sending you.

_____

_____

_____

_____

_____

_____

_____

_____

_____

_____

Indulgent Experiences

One great way to nurture our self-worth is to take a simple thing and turn it into an experience. Too often, we take simple things for granted and don't realize how they can enhance our day and how we see ourselves. Today, take a simple pleasure that you enjoy (taking a bath, drinking a cup of coffee or tea, driving, etc.) and turn it into a fun, indulgent experience. Some examples include:

- Adding a small piece of chocolate to your coffee and sipping it slowly while listening to your favorite music.

- Using bath bombs or shower steamers and lighting candles while you bathe.

- Driving to work on back roads instead of the highway, with the windows open.

- Finding silk or satin sheets (or anything you find cozy) for your bed for extra luxurious sleeping.

- Eat lunch outside (weather permitting, of course).

When we're stressed and overwhelmed, nurturing ourselves is more critical than ever. But often, we react poorly when we're under stress. How can you remember to nurture yourself when you're feeling stressed? This could be calling a friend to talk, listening to soothing music, or leaving work early. Make a list of some go-tos that would work for you. The next time you're feeling overwhelmed, return to this page to remind yourself how to release the stress.

I love who I am and who I am becoming.

When we have low self-esteem, we often do or say things just to please others. What are you doing just to please others or even society at large? Think of all the ways that you may be "people pleasing." What can you do or say to react more in line with your authentic self? Write down some ideas for responses that would work in your typical people-pleasing situations.

_____

_____

_____

_____

_____

_____

_____

_____

_____

_____

Mirror Practice

For this exercise, I'm inviting you to stand in front of a mirror and recite affirmations to yourself. It may make you feel uncomfortable at first because you're not used to looking at yourself for long periods or perhaps you're not used to saying kind things to yourself. Remember, it is okay to be uncomfortable—you're trying something new and working toward growth!

Feel free to use the affirmations throughout this journal or make your own to use. Here's how to use them:

1. Stand in front of a mirror. Relax and take a deep breath.
2. Make eye contact and state your affirmation clearly.
3. Repeat this affirmation with confidence.
4. Try your best to recite affirmations to yourself for at least five minutes. If you can do it for longer, even better!

Far too often, we have things in our lives that are merely taking up space or energy and don't enrich our lives. These can be personal possessions, thought patterns, or even people. When these things occupy space in our lives, we may not have room for more of the things that enrich us, like self-love. What can you get rid of to make room for nurturing yourself?

_____

_____

_____

_____

_____

_____

_____

_____

_____

_____

_____

Music is a powerful means to help us express ourselves and give our spirits a boost. Think about all the songs that make you feel powerful, confident, and self-assured. Write them down below and reflect on exactly how they make you feel. Now put them into a playlist to listen to anytime you need a boost to your self-worth. (You can also share this playlist with a friend to spread the good vibes!)

_____

_____

_____

_____

_____

_____

_____

_____

_____

_____

_____

Dress for Confidence

We all have certain clothes or accessories that make us feel like a million bucks when we wear them. It might be because it's in our favorite color, it represents a part of our personality, or it always fits just right.

Today, wear that piece of clothing or accessory that makes you feel great. Notice how your mood changes when you wear it. Notice how your confidence increases.

You may have more than one piece of clothing or accessory that makes you feel this way. If you do, figure out how you can incorporate them into your daily dress so you can always have an extra bit of confidence when you walk out the door.

Sleeping habits have a lot to do with nurturing yourself. How often have you awakened after only getting a few hours of sleep and dreaded the day ahead of you? We've all been there. Your body is tired from not getting enough rest, and your mood is affected, too. How are your sleeping habits helping or hindering how you nurture yourself? What are some steps you can take to enhance your sleep?

_____

_____

_____

_____

_____

_____

_____

_____

_____

_____

_____

Giving ourselves compliments is a rarity for most of us. Usually, we rely on someone else to acknowledge us in that way. Instead of waiting for someone to compliment you, do it yourself! Toot your own horn below and write at least five sincere compliments to yourself. The next time you're feeling down, come back to this prompt and read what you wrote. Feel free to add more compliments, too, each time you come back.

What's Your Love Language?

If you're not familiar with the "five love languages," they are thought to be the primary ways people express love to others and want love expressed to them. They include:

- Words of affirmation
- Quality time
- Physical touch
- Acts of service
- Receiving gifts (these do not need to be tangible items)

You may resonate with some of these ways to express love more than others, but we need them all. This includes showing all these types of love to yourself! How can you use these love languages to nurture yourself? Write down one thing you can do for each type of love language below.

Words of affirmation: _____

Quality time: _____

Physical touch: _____

Acts of service: _____

Receiving gifts: _____

You can also head to the Resources section (page 158) to find out more about the five love languages, if you're interested.

I no longer choose to believe in old limitations and lack. I now choose to begin to see myself as the Universe sees me—perfect, whole, and complete.

—Louise Hay

Celebrating ourselves doesn't always have to be huge (though it should be, on occasion!). What are some simple ways you can celebrate yourself or show yourself some appreciation? Reflect and brainstorm on this. Then follow through on a few of them—you deserve it.

_____

_____

_____

_____

_____

_____

_____

_____

_____

_____

Love Letter

A simple but powerful way to nurture your self-worth is to write yourself a letter. Think of it as a love letter to yourself. It could be as straightforward or as creative as you would like. All you need to get started is a pen, paper, and a couple of positive thoughts.

Sit and reflect. Try to pinpoint different aspects of yourself that you love—mentally, physically, spiritually, and emotionally. Brag about yourself. If you'd like, decorate your love letter with stickers, markers, or anything else that would make it a positive experience for you. Whenever you're feeling down, take out your letter to remind yourself of all of your positive attributes.

We all need a little inspiration now and then. Learning how to nurture yourself can be tricky (that's why you bought this journal!). In the lines below, write down things that inspire you to nurture yourself. These things can be people, quotes, affirmations, favorite books, etc. Do a little research if you need ideas for your inspiration. When you need an extra push to continue to nurture yourself, come back to this prompt.

_____

_____

_____

_____

_____

_____

_____

_____

_____

_____

_____

You're probably really busy the majority of time with work, school, family commitments, being a good friend, and everything in between. When you have a day off from all of that, how do you spend it? Are you more intentional with what you do? In what ways can you practice self-care on your days off?

_____

_____

_____

_____

_____

_____

_____

_____

_____

_____

_____

On page 96, you wrote down ways you can celebrate yourself. Now let's talk about your achievements! Write down all the achievements that you can remember. Nothing is too big, too small, or too long ago. Did you win the fifth-grade spelling bee? Did you recently get a promotion? Write it down. Anytime you need a boost, come back to this page and remember all that you've done so far, and add to it as you go.

_____

_____

_____

_____

_____

_____

_____

_____

_____

_____

_____

Lovely Masterpiece

Get creative and surround yourself with love!

1. Grab some paper and something to draw with.

2. Draw a picture of yourself in the middle of the paper. Feel free to be as detailed and creative as you want with your drawing.

3. Surround your picture with kind and loving words. If you've already written yourself a letter (page 97), you can go back to that letter and pick out some key phrases that are especially empowering for you.

4. After you've completed your masterpiece, hang it somewhere you can glance at it every day. When you see it, you'll be reminded that you are surrounded by love, even when it doesn't feel like it.

Building on a previous prompt, we don't need to wait for a day off to nurture ourselves. We should take care of ourselves a little bit every day, even when it seems impossible to fit into our schedule. What are ways you can carve some nurturing into your life? For example, you could say positive affirmations to yourself while you're commuting to or from work. What others can you think of and how can you implement them into your routine?

Imagine one year into the future. You've been cultivating self-love and nurturing yourself. You're embracing who you are and thriving. You've even found some good teachings in your failures and mistakes. Write down what your life looks like in this scenario. How does it feel to know that this could be your future?

_____

_____

_____

_____

_____

_____

_____

_____

_____

_____

_____

I find the best way to love someone is not to change them, but instead, help them reveal the greatest version of themselves.

—Steve Maraboli

Reflect Your True Value

Y ou've probably heard sayings about how our relationships are a reflection of who we are. While this belief doesn't hold true with every single relationship in your life, (your next-door neighbor probably doesn't have much effect on how you view yourself), it can be highly accurate for your most significant relationships.

Self-esteem relates to your inner thoughts and beliefs. These beliefs are manifested in our actions. And through these actions, we show others how we want to be treated and valued. You have the right to choose what you do; however, your choice will reflect and inform others on what they can do.

Whether you choose to set boundaries, stand up for yourself, let go of relationships that are no longer serving you, or anything in between, this section is all about showing others that you know you're amazing and deserve respect.

Our relationships are often central to who we are as people. Because they are so vital to us, they affect both how we behave and how we see ourselves. What are your current significant relationships like? These relationships could be with family members, close friends, work colleagues, mentors, etc. Reflect on and describe your role in these relationships. How do these relationships affect what you do or how you see yourself?

_____

_____

_____

_____

_____

_____

_____

_____

_____

_____

_____

We may show others that we value ourselves without realizing it. What are some ways that you have shown people how you value yourself recently? For example, did you speak up in a meeting at work or tell someone that you didn't want to go on a date with them? Write about these times. When you need a confidence boost, read about all the times you demonstrated how you value yourself.

We may try to hide part of ourselves because we're not sure how our true selves will affect our relationships. Have you tried to hide part of yourself because of your relationships with others? For example, you might be uncomfortable discussing your relationships, so you never bring a significant other to family functions. How does hiding this part of yourself make you feel? What do you lose out on? What steps could you take to make yourself more comfortable with sharing?

Take Up Space

When we have low self-esteem, we will sometimes shrink or hide, both literally and figuratively. Practicing taking up space can help you build confidence and present yourself confidently. Cultivate the art of "putting yourself out there." Here are a few ways:

- If you usually wear accessories (hat, sunglasses, etc.) to hide, do without them for a day.
- Conversely, if you don't wear accessories but want to, try it for a day.
- Tell someone your opinion when they ask for it.
- Stand instead of sitting if appropriate for the situation.
- Make eye contact when talking to someone.
- If someone says something that bothers you, respectfully tell them.
- Stretch out your legs and arms when sitting.

This can all be done with respect—taking up space doesn't mean encroaching on the space of others. You're entitled to be there, too!

When I value myself,
I show others how I want to be
treated and valued.

On page 106, you wrote about some of your current significant relationships. After spending time thinking about these relationships, do you feel that they are healthy? If so, what is beneficial about them? If not, what needs to change to make them healthier?

_____

_____

_____

_____

_____

_____

_____

_____

_____

_____

_____

We all make assumptions about others. This does not make us bad people. However, it is a wonderful practice to try to challenge our assumptions. Are there any assumptions that you believe people make about you? What are these assumptions based on? How can you challenge them?

_____

_____

_____

_____

_____

_____

_____

_____

_____

_____

_____

Mindful Interactions

Does your energy shift depending on the situation you're in or the people you're with? It's natural that some people will drain your energy and others will energize you. Think about all the interactions you've had in the past week. Who left you feeling content, happy, or excited? Who left you feeling tired or cranky?

Consider steps you can take to maximize or minimize the time spent with them. Here are some examples:

- Make a monthly or weekly plan to spend time with someone who leaves you feeling energized.
- Text or email people you want to minimize time with instead of calling or participating in in-person meetings.
- Create boundaries with people who leave you feeling negatively.
- Get a group of your favorite people together and bask in the love.

The way we were raised can greatly affect how we see and value ourselves. What would you like to tell your parents or caregivers about how they raised you to value yourself? Reflect and write about it. Would you feel comfortable sharing this with them now? You can also reflect on how your values have changed from that time, and how and why that happened.

_____

_____

_____

_____

_____

_____

_____

_____

_____

_____

_____

_____

Impactful Letters

Our relationships have a tremendous impact on how we value ourselves and even how we react to others' perceptions of us. In a previous exercise, you practiced writing a letter to yourself (page 97). Let's expand on this concept and write a letter to someone else. The experience can often be as freeing as talking to them in person. Additionally, you don't have to worry about saying the right words or being judged in the moment.

Think of people who have impacted you in your life in significant ways. Write a letter to one of these people, letting them know how they've influenced how you value yourself (positively or negatively).

Afterward, reflect on how you feel. If you feel comfortable, you can give this person the letter you've written or just keep it as a reminder to yourself.

Have you ever done something just because someone else wanted you to do it or to impress someone that you liked? We've all been there, but it might not always be worth it. What's the most outrageous or unlikely thing that you've done just to please someone? If you could do it over again, would you? Why or why not? What can you learn (good or bad) from this experience?

_____

_____

_____

_____

_____

_____

_____

_____

_____

_____

_____

In addition to setting boundaries with others, sometimes we need to set clear boundaries with ourselves. Have you ever told yourself you're not going to do something (like stay up until 3 a.m. when you have to be up at 7 a.m.) only to do it anyway? That's an example of how we might violate our own boundary. What boundaries do you need to set up with yourself? How can you make sure you'll stick to them?

_____

_____

_____

_____

_____

_____

_____

_____

_____

_____

_____

_____

Setting Boundaries

Creating firm boundaries is a powerful way to show others how they should treat us and how we want to be valued. Even though we have a right to them, creating and holding those boundaries can be incredibly difficult. Think of three people that you need to develop better boundaries with and write their names below. What limits can you create with them to protect your value? For example:

Name: *My manager*

Boundary: *I will not answer her phone calls after I leave work.*

Boundary: *I will only have a meeting without 24 hours' notice if it is an emergency.*

Name: _____

Boundary: _____

Boundary: _____

Name: _____

Boundary: _____

Boundary: _____

Name: _____

Boundary: _____

Boundary: _____

Valuing ourselves can lead to feelings of guilt because we think it's selfish. The more you value yourself, the more you can also show others you value them and even support them in valuing themselves. You don't have to feel guilty about valuing yourself. What else don't you need to feel guilty about? Write your thoughts in the space provided.

_____

_____

_____

_____

_____

_____

_____

_____

_____

_____

_____

Mutual caring relationships require kindness and patience, tolerance, optimism, joy in the other's achievements, confidence in oneself, and the ability to give without undue thought of gain.

—Fred Rogers

We all have traits or parts of ourselves that we want others to appreciate. This could be our intelligence, sense of style, or ability to bake the perfect cookies. What would you like others to see in you? How can you express your gifts more clearly so others are able to appreciate them?

_____

_____

_____

_____

_____

_____

_____

_____

_____

_____

_____

_____

When working on our self-esteem, we may have more negative views of ourselves than others do. It can also be hard for us to decipher how we are seen and valued by others, so think about asking others for their thoughts. What trusted people could you ask about how they perceive you? Once you've figured out who to ask, write down your plan for making the connection.

_____

_____

_____

_____

_____

_____

_____

_____

_____

_____

_____

Challenging Assumptions

In an earlier prompt, we talked about assumptions that we make about people (page 112). Now we're going to do a similar exercise to help bring about more awareness about the assumptions we make about others. Remember, making assumptions doesn't make us bad people, but we can challenge them.

1. Go somewhere where you can observe people and they can observe you. This could be a mall, park, or grocery store.

2. As you're looking around at people, what do you notice about them? You might notice how they look, how they carry themselves, how they interact with others, or the things they're doing.

3. How can you challenge your assumptions about them?

    The next time you make an assumption, try going through this process again to challenge how you think about others, or even yourself.

Sometimes we miss the mark when trying to show others that we value them. If we reflect on how we show others that we value them, we can be sure they get the right message—we can also come to understand how we want to be treated. In what ways do you think your loved ones want to be valued? How do you show or express how you value them? Whenever you're unsure how to show someone you value them, revisit this list.

_____

_____

_____

_____

_____

_____

_____

_____

_____

_____

_____

Even if it may not always seem like it, people value your opinion. What do you often have people asking your advice about? Maybe it's fashion, the best way to train a dog, or personal finance tips. Write about your experiences. The next time you feel as if people don't value what you have to say, come back to this prompt and remember all the times people wanted to know your thoughts.

_____

_____

_____

_____

_____

_____

_____

_____

_____

_____

_____

Your Value

The main goal of this section is to help you think about how you want to show people your value. While we may be clear on how much we value ourselves, we sometimes need to act to effectively show it to others.

In the space below, write what you'd like to be valued for and specifically how you are going to show that valuable quality to others.

MY VALUABLE QUALITIES	HOW I WILL SHOW THEM
EX. *SELF-CONFIDENCE*	*I WILL SHARE MY IDEAS DURING MEETINGS.*

Is there someone in your life you really admire or look up to? It's completely okay to want to be more like someone else, but you can also look up to and admire yourself by focusing on the qualities that you possess. Who do you aspire to be more like? What qualities or skills do they have that you'd like to have more of? What steps can you take to build on these qualities for yourself?

Our relationships with other people are among the most critical aspects of our lives. It's hard to go through life without relationships. We all deserve to have relationships that are loving and kind. What does your ideal relationship look like? How are you able to be yourself and be valued in this relationship? What is the ideal level of give and take? (Note: This doesn't need to be a romantic relationship.)

Cultivate Love

While valuing ourselves has to start within us, cultivating that value can be supported when we surround ourselves with people who love and care for us and who we love in return.

1. Draw a picture of yourself in the middle of the space below.

2. Around you, draw all the people who help you see your value. Stick figures are totally fine here! You can even just write their names if you prefer.

3. Complete the artwork by writing positive words that you associate with these loved ones and your relationships with them.

Now more than ever, YOU can do this, it can be all yours. And left to your own devices, you can find YOUR VOICE.

—Dave Grohl

Harness Your Inner Power

All the work you've done so far has been building up to this. You're establishing your true self, leaning into self-compassion and self-respect, learning from failures, nurturing your mind, body, and soul, and showing others how to value you.

Now is the time to harness all that goodness and power. This power will help you love yourself; it will also allow you to accomplish your dreams and lead a thriving life. Once you're confident in yourself—including who you are, your abilities, and your relationships—life opens up in ways that seemed impossible before. You'll find yourself wanting to experience more and empower others, and you'll be immensely capable of picking yourself up whenever you get knocked down.

Before you start on the next prompt, imagine all that you can be and what you can accomplish now that you are ready to step into your power. Take all of those dreams with you while you finish this section. Let's do this!

Page 131 gave you a taste of what stepping into your power could mean and look like. But it's up to you to define what "stepping into your power" is. Take a few minutes to think about that phrase. What does it mean to you? When it feels like stepping into your power is too much, reflect back on this definition and know that it can change as you do.

_____

_____

_____

_____

_____

_____

_____

_____

_____

_____

You've made major changes and progress in your self-esteem journey. What do you consider to be your biggest achievement in your journey so far? How do you feel about this achievement? Why is it important to you?

_____

_____

_____

_____

_____

_____

_____

_____

_____

_____

_____

We've talked a lot about embracing who you are. Now is a good time to think about your future. Who do you want to be? Write about your goals and aspirations. For example, say you want to be a public speaker to share your story with others. What steps can you take toward reaching your goal? In the example of public speaking, a step could be taking a public speaking class.

_____

_____

_____

_____

_____

_____

_____

_____

_____

_____

_____

Once you've started stepping into your power, you can start building a life that you love. But what does this mean to you? Think about it, and then write about what living a life you love potentially means to you. Revisit this often and continue letting your vision take form through your words on paper and actions in life. If you don't have a blank journal, this is a great time to get one as your thoughts begin to overflow these pages.

_____

_____

_____

_____

_____

_____

_____

_____

_____

_____

_____

Celebrate Your Accomplishments

Think about your biggest accomplishment to date or just your most significant accomplishment this week. What was it? How did you celebrate? If you did celebrate, congratulations! You deserve it! Think about how you can keep this celebration going.

If you didn't celebrate, this exercise is your invitation. Go as big or as intimate as you'd like. Seriously. Get a cake and throw a party, or get your favorite takeout and a cupcake with a candle. Consider how you can celebrate yourself more often, even just because.

Stepping into our power can be scary and can sometimes make us want to retreat inside ourselves instead. Doing new things and being a newer, brighter version of yourself is a significant change. What makes you fearful or apprehensive about stepping into your power? What can you do to lessen that angst?

_____

_____

_____

_____

_____

_____

_____

_____

_____

_____

You've learned a lot about building your self-esteem and cultivating self-love by using this journal. Knowing what you know now, what's your self-love mission moving forward? How do you plan on fulfilling it? For example, your mission could be to practice an act of self-love every day.

_____

_____

_____

_____

_____

_____

_____

_____

_____

_____

_____

I am confident that I can handle whatever life brings my way.

The more confident we feel in ourselves, the more things we want to do, see, and experience. Because of your increased sense of self-worth, what are you looking forward to? Remember, not even the sky's the limit now. Write about the possibilities that come to mind in all areas of life. Make a plan to try to do one thing each week that you've been looking forward to.

_____

_____

_____

_____

_____

_____

_____

_____

_____

_____

What Are Your Goals?

In the space below, write down things you want to do in the left column and why you want to do them in the right column. Understanding why you're doing something helps clarify the intent behind it, so you know if you are doing it for yourself or for an external reason. Either reason is valid, but it's important to understand what is driving you and if it's an authentic desire.

Your "whys" can be as simple or as complicated as you want them to be. You can also have multiple "whys." Here's an example to help get you started.

WHAT I WANT TO DO	WHY I WANT TO DO IT
EX. *WRITE A BOOK*	*I'VE ALWAYS WANTED TO SHARE MY ORIGINAL RECIPES.*

Low self-esteem stops us from doing things that we want to do. It might be because we're worried that we're not good enough to succeed or we don't want to fail. What's something your self-esteem has hindered you from doing? Are you ready to try it now? Why or why not? If not, what steps are you ready to take to move toward that point?

_____

_____

_____

_____

_____

_____

_____

_____

_____

_____

_____

Powerful Words

Words can hold a lot of power for us. Now that you've worked through these sections, choose three words that connect you to your inner power. Think of words that describe your journey or what you have discovered about yourself. Write the words below and reflect on how they are connected to your inner power or what they mean to you.

The following words to help get your creative juices flowing (you don't have to use these words, but you can if they deeply resonate with you): brave, expansion, tenacious, joyful, miracle, endure.

Now write your three words on three separate sticky notes. Place them in spots where you can see them often. Change them or add more whenever new "power words" inspire you.

Sometimes harnessing our own inner power can inspire others to do the same. How can you empower others to use their own inner power? This could be by sharing your story, encouraging others, or making an impact in your community. After writing about how you can empower those around you, brainstorm one or two steps you can take to move forward.

Breaking unhelpful routines can help us step into our power. The more power we feel like we have, the more we can stop doing things that no longer serve us. What routines do you have that limit your ability to thrive in life? An unhelpful routine might be scrolling through social media for hours instead of going to sleep. How can you start breaking your less-helpful routines?

Reach Your Goals

One of the best ways to meet a goal is to break it into smaller chunks.

Think of your larger goal as the top of a ladder and the smaller chunks as rungs on the ladder. You have to get to the first rung before you can climb to the second. Take one of your goals and figure out the steps it might take to get there. You can even jot them down, one on top of another.

Visualize yourself going up the ladder to reach your goal. See yourself grasping each rung of the ladder and pulling yourself up bit by bit. Imagine yourself reaching your goal and celebrating your win. Whenever your goal feels as if it is too far away, remember this visualization. Each step you take is progress.

One of the best metaphors for stepping into your power is the sun. It rises every day, glows with warmth, and sets every night, satisfied that it has provided all it can. How can you embody the sun as you continue on this journey? What is one thing that you can do each day that will leave you feeling satisfied at day's end?

Visualize Your Life

As you step more confidently into your new life, what would you like to do with it? Visualize what you'd like to do, feeling more self-assured and ready to step into your inner power.

Creating a vision board seems simple, but can be a powerful exercise. Grab some supplies, like stickers, scissors, pens, glue, and magazines. Envision what you want your life to be moving forward. If you see something that fits that vision, stick it to this page. (If you need more space, use a separate piece of paper or create something digitally through Pinterest or a graphic design program.)

Your life is your story, and the adventure ahead of you is the journey to fulfill your own purpose and potential.

—Kerry Washington

We are all granted talents and expertise in different areas. That's part of what makes each of us unique, interesting, and capable of excelling. What do you excel at? This isn't the space to be modest! To springboard off your talents, how can you plan on using them in the future? Write about the possibilities in the space below.

We all have a comfort zone that we like to live in most of the time. Has your comfort zone changed as you've learned more about yourself? You might realize that you're speaking more during work meetings or wearing clothes that you might not have worn before. Where is your comfort zone now compared to before you started using this journal? What are some ways you can celebrate moving toward a new comfort zone?

Fill Your Cup

You've probably heard the saying about your glass being half full or half empty, depending on how you look at it. That's true to an extent, but let's think about it differently: If your cup is full of negativity or things that no longer serve you, having a full cup isn't ideal. However, if your cup is full of positive things, like loving relationships and high self-esteem, having a cup that's half full might not be so bad.

Instead of your glass being half full or half empty, draw a cup or mug and write down what your glass is full of in the space below. This glass is yours to fill. You get to decide how full it is, and you can refill it whenever you wish.

One of the most rewarding things we can do in the world is harness our inner strengths to help others. This will look different for everyone. One person might want to support youth with their education, and someone else might want to look after the environment. What impact would you like to make in your community or in the world? What's one step you could take to start making an impact today?

Look back at everything you've written in this journal. Take as long as you'd like to absorb it. What have you learned about yourself? About self-esteem? How will you use this knowledge moving forward? What more do you want to do for yourself in this area?

_____

_____

_____

_____

_____

_____

_____

_____

_____

_____

_____

Step into Your Power

Stepping into your power is an empowering, transformative experience and deserves to be celebrated.

What you'll need:

- Comfortable clothes
- A silent, calming environment (or you can play music that soothes you)
- A candle (if you don't have a candle, visualizing one can work just as well)
- This journal

Instructions:

1. Once you're in your calm environment, light your candle.
2. Think about everything you've accomplished on your self-love journey so far.
3. Repeat the following affirmations or your own words:

   I love myself more and more each day.
   I am empowered to go even further.
   Today, I step into my power.

4. Continue to reflect on your journey and repeat the affirmations for as long as you need.
5. When you're ready, blow out your candle.

A Final Word

Congratulations on making it to this point! Everything you've written, drawn, thought about, and practiced has led you to where you are now.

Working through the six sections of this journal shows how dedicated you are to increasing your self-esteem. That dedication is power; an act of self-love, which is the combination of self-esteem along with self-awareness, self-worth, and self-care. You already know what self-esteem is, so let's take a brief look at the other three.

Self-awareness is the practice of being aware of your thought processes and emotions and why they may cause you to act the way you do. Many of the journaling prompts examined your thought processes and emotions. **Self-worth** is closely connected to self-esteem. It is about how we feel about ourselves, but it also encompasses our inherent worth. This means there is nothing you have to do to be worthy. You just are. And **self-care** is the things we do that keep us healthy—emotionally, mentally, and physically. Many of the exercises presented were acts of self-care because they were actionable. For example, the exercise on self-soothing touches on page 33 is an act of self-care. It is often much easier to do something than it is to change your beliefs and mindset.

All of these qualities go hand in hand and influence one another. Throughout this journal, you've been practicing bits and pieces of each of these things. You may even recognize that you do less in one area than in another. Having and practicing all of these methods will help you thrive in all areas of your life, no matter what life throws at you.

The resources on the following pages will help you continue on your journey of cultivating self-esteem. It is essential to continually learn and seek out support because we cannot do it all alone; nor should we have to.

No matter where you started and where you are now, you deserve an enormous round of applause. What you did isn't easy, and you deserve every bit of happiness coming your way. You always did, but hopefully now you believe it.

Resources

BOOKS

The Ayurvedic Self-Care Handbook BY SARAH KUCERA
Based on the principles of Ayurveda, an Indian holistic healing method, this book provides rituals that you can do in less than 10 minutes to help enhance your mind, body, and spirit.

Big Magic BY ELIZABETH GILBERT
There is powerful magic in our lives that anyone can tap into: creativity. This book will help you explore your creativity and use it to live a more fulfilling life.

The 5 Love Languages BY GARY CHAPMAN
This book will help you learn how you and others feel loved and provides actionable tips to build better relationships.

The Gifts of Imperfection BY BRENÉ BROWN
Living an "imperfect" life may not be as bad as it is perceived. This book provides hope, support, and guidance to anyone seeking more meaning and gratitude in their lives.

Self-Care Journal for Young Adults BY BRIANA HOLLIS
Explore self-care through a multifaceted lens. This journal will help you expand your thinking about self-care and develop new self-care practices.

Untamed BY GLENNON DOYLE
This memoir chronicles the struggles of wanting to be all things to everyone and discovering that we all need to trust in ourselves to live authentically.

The following Instagram accounts were created by people who wanted to inspire others to build self-esteem and find joy in being ourselves.

DOMONIQUE ROBINSON: @TheSelfCareMentor

JESS EDEN: @Happily.Jessie

MICHELLE GOODLOE: @TheGMichelle

A SELF-LOVE COMMUNITY: @TheSelfLoveBlossom

LACRISHA HOLCOMB: @TherapyIsLight

The following websites will help you continue your self-esteem journey. They provide inspiration, advice, information, and more on creating a fulfilling life rooted in self-love and self-compassion.

ALWAYS WELL WITHIN: AlwaysWellWithin.com

BLESSING MANIFESTING: BlessingManifesting.com

THE BLISSFUL MIND: TheBlissfulMind.com

DWELL IN MAGIC: JessicaDimas.com

PSYCHOLOGY TODAY (FIND A THERAPIST): PsychologyToday.com/us/therapists

References

Brown, Brené. *Daring Greatly: How the Courage to Be Vulnerable Transforms the Way We Live, Love, Parent, and Lead.* New York: Avery, 2015.

Chapman, Gary. *The 5 Love Languages: The Secret to Love That Lasts.* Chicago: Northfield Publishing, 2015.

Cherry, Kendra. "What Is Self-Esteem?" Verywell Mind. Accessed May 7, 2021. VerywellMind.com/what-is-self-esteem-2795868.

"Dave Grohl's SXSW Keynote Speech: The Complete Text." *Rolling Stone.* March 15, 2013. RollingStone.com/music/music-news/dave-grohls-sxsw-keynote-speech -the-complete-text-89152.

Germer, Christopher K. *The Mindful Path to Self-Compassion: Freeing Yourself from Destructive Thoughts and Emotions.* New York: Guilford Press, 2009.

Hale, Mandy. *The Single Woman: Life, Love, and a Dash of Sass.* Nashville: Thomas Nelson, 2013.

Hanh, Thich Nhat. *The Art of Power.* New York: HarperOne, 2007.

Hay, Louise. *You Can Heal Your Life.* Carlsbad, CA: Hay House, Inc., 1984.

Kornfield, Jack. *Buddha's Little Instruction Book.* New York: Bantam Books, 1994.

Maraboli, Steve. *Unapologetically You: Reflections on Life and the Human Experience.* Port Washington, NY: A Better Today, 2013.

"Neil Gaiman: Keynote Address 2012." University of the Arts. May 17, 2012. UArts.edu /neil-gaiman-keynote-address-2012.

Newcomb, Alyssa. "Kerry Washington: 'Scandal' Star Shares Memories from Her College Years." ABC News. ABC News Network. May 19, 2013. ABCNews.Go.com /Entertainment/kerry-washington-scandal-star-honorary-doctorate-george -washington/story?id=19211377.

Quindlen, Anna. "1999 Mount Holyoke Commencement Speech." James Clear. Accessed on November 25, 2020. JamesClear.com/great-speeches/1999-mount-holyoke -commencement-speech-by-anna-quindlen.

Rogers, Fred. *The World According to Mister Rogers: Important Things to Remember*. New York: Hachette Books, 2003.

"Self-esteem Declines Sharply among Older Adults While Middle-Aged Are Most Confident." American Psychological Association. April 2010. APA.org/news /press/releases/2010/04/self-esteem.

"The First Lady Speaks at King College Prep High School's Commencement." The White House: President Barack Obama. National Archives and Records Administration. June 11, 2015. ObamaWhiteHouse.Archives.gov/photos-and-video/video/2015 /06/11/first-lady-speaks-king-college-prep-high-schools-commencement.

Acknowledgments

The funny thing is, I put writing a book on my bucket list in late 2020 (technically, two books). Here I am less than a year later, with both under my belt.

First, I want to give huge thanks to my family. Without them, I wouldn't be where I am now. Thank you for the movie nights, game nights, and home-cooked meals that kept me going.

To my work colleagues, thank you for being just as excited as I was when I told you about my writing adventures. I deeply appreciate all of you.

Lastly, many thanks to Samantha Holland, Patty Consolazio, Ann Edwards and the entire team at Callisto Media. It has been a pleasure working with you over the past few months.

About the Author

Briana Hollis, LSW, is a licensed social worker and self-care coach based in Cleveland, Ohio. After graduating from Case Western Reserve University, she has spent her career supporting students and clients in college access, crisis intervention, and mental health. Her passion for helping others spurred her to create this journal and the *Self-Care Journal for Young Adults*.

When she's not working, she loves spending time with loved ones, traveling the world, and learning everything about the latest Marvel movie.

You can connect more with Briana on Instagram @LearningToBeFreeBlog or through her website at LearningToBeFree.com, where she shares best practices on being a person and building a life that you love.

CPSIA information can be obtained
at www.ICGtesting.com
Printed in the USA
JSHW052009190921
18781JS00002B/2